ISBN 978-0-656-60070-0
PIBN 11289080

This book is a reproduction of an important historical work. Forgotten Books uses
state-of-the-art technology to digitally reconstruct the work, preserving the original format
whilst repairing imperfections present in the aged copy. In rare cases, an imperfection in
the original, such as a blemish or missing page, may be replicated in our edition. We do,
however, repair the vast majority of imperfections successfully; any imperfections that
remain are intentionally left to preserve the state of such historical works.

Historic, archived document

Do not assume content reflects current
scientific knowledge, policies, or practices.

February, 1945

CREAM

Questions and Answers Relating to
War Food Order 13
(revised)

This statement prepared for general distribution is
intended to supply the answers to some of the questions
regarding War Food Order 13. In the interests of simplicity,
answers are in some cases abbreviated to the extent that
they are incomplete in a technical sense. The Order itself
should always be consulted where a specific problem is
involved. For additional information write to the Order
Administrator, War Food Order 13, Office of Marketing
Services, War Food Administration, Washington 25, D. C.

General Questions

1. Q. What is WFO 13?

   A. WFO 13 commonly known as the cream order, is an order issued
   by the War Food Administration restricting the distribution and
   use of cream and related products and the manufacture of filled
   cream.

2. Q. When was WFO 13 issued?

   A. WFO 13 was first issued on February 2, 1943. It was preceded
   by Conservation Order M-259 issued by the War Production Board
   on November 25, 1942. Amendments to WFO 13 have been issued,
   the most recent one being Amendment 5, dated February 6, 1945.

3. Q. What is the purpose of the Order?

   A. The purpose is to conserve the Nation's supply of butterfat and
   fluid milk so that both may be utilized in those channels where
   the need is most urgent, from the standpoint of war necessity.

4. Q. What products are affected by the Order?

   A. Cream, cream products, and filled cream.

5. Q. How is "cream" defined?

   A. "Cream" is defined broadly to include the product in all its forms. For the full definition, the Order should be consulted.

6. Q. What is a "cream product"?

   A. "Cream product" is defined as cream to which there has been added a culture, stabilizer, sugar, salt, condiments, spices, flavoring, or similar ingredients.

7. Q. What is "filled cream"?

   A. "Filled cream" means any milk, cream, or skim milk, to which there has been added any fat or oil other than milk fat, so that the resulting product is an imitation of cream, provided that it has a total content of all oil and fat, including milk fat, in excess of 19 percent.

8. Q. How is the term "handler" defined?

   A. "Handler" means (a) any person who engages in the business of transporting or processing milk or cream, or of manufacturing any dairy product, or (b) any person who produces filled cream for sale as such or for use as an ingredient in the manufacture or preparation of food products for sale. Such term does not include persons such as peddlers, vendors, or retail stores, who merely deliver milk or cream to consumers.

9. Q. What is meant by the terms "milk fat" and "milk solids" as used in the Order?

   A. "Milk fat" means "butterfat". "Milk solids" means the total solids of milk and consists of milk fat and milk solids-not-fat.

Cream and Cream Products

10. Q. What restrictions does the Order impose on the sale or delivery of cream and cream products?

    A. The Order prohibits any person from delivering, except to a handler, any cream or cream product having a milk fat content in excess of 19 percent, except in those States where the minimum test required by State law exceeds 19 percent. Cream sold in such States may exceed the minimum State butterfat test by 1 percent.

The Order also prohibits any person from delivering, except to a handler, any cream or cream product to which there has been added evaporated milk, condensed milk, dried whole milk, or dried skim milk.

Q. What restrictions does the Order impose on the use of cream or cream products?

A. The Order provides that no handler shall use any cream or cream product having a milk fat content in excess of 19 percent, except in the processing of milk or cream, or in the manufacture of a dairy product, or in the production of filled cream.

An exception, similar to that cited in answer to the previous question, is provided for those States where the minimum test required exceeds 18 percent.

Q. Is there any provision whereby restaurants and others who are not handlers under the Order may obtain heavy cream for use in making ice cream?

A. Yes. The Order provides that any person may sell or deliver to any restaurant, hotel, bakery, or similar establishment any cream or cream product, regardless of its milk fat content, if the purchaser certifies in writing to the seller that such cream or cream product is to be used in the manufacture of frozen dairy foods.

Q. Is any provision made whereby doctors may prescribe heavy cream for their patients?

A. Yes. Persons under supervised medical treatment and institutions engaged in the care and treatment of the sick are entitled to receive heavy cream from a handler, provided the handler is supplied with a prescription from the patient's physician or a responsible official of the institution specifying the following:

    1. The milk fat content of cream required for such use;

    2. The daily quantity needed;

    3. Certification as to the necessity of such cream for supervised medical treatment.

Such written statement is not valid for obtaining such cream unless approved by a public health officer who is a physician, or by the secretary of a county medical society.

Filled Cream

14.   Q: What restrictions does the Order impose with respect to filled cream?

      A.   The Order provides that no handler shall, during any calendar month, utilize in the production of filled cream a quantity of milk solids in excess of 75 percent of his monthly base.

15.   Q.   What is the base period used in determining a handler's monthly base?

      A.   The base period is (1) the month of May 1944 in the case of a handler who produced filled cream during that month and who produced less than 100 gallons of filled cream during any calendar month from April 1943 through March 1944; and (2) the period from April 1943 to March 1944, inclusive, for all other handlers.

16.   Q.   What is a handler's monthly base?

      A.   The monthly base, applicable to any calendar month, means (1) for a handler whose base period is May 1944, the pounds of milk solids utilized by him in the production of filled cream during such base period; and (2) for a handler whose base period is the period from April 1, 1943, to March 31, 1944, inclusive, the pounds of milk solids utilized by him in the production of filled cream during the corresponding calendar month of the base period.

Case Questions

17.   Q.   Will the fact that a handler is not equipped to test his cream for its butterfat content excuse him from complying with the Order?

      A.   No. Compliance is required of all handlers. Small-size Babcock testers are relatively inexpensive. Also, small operators can effectively control the butterfat test of cream produced if they know the average butterfat test of their milk and adjust the volume of cream accordingly. A table for this purpose may be obtained by writing to the Order Administrator.

18. Q. Can a handler deliver cream or cream products which test in excess of 19 percent butterfat to a manufacturer of cream puffs, cream pies, or similar products?

     A. No. Heavy cream may be delivered only to a handler, and a manufacturer of candy or bakery goods is not construed to be a handler as defined by the Order.

19. Q. Will it be sufficient for a medical certificate to state that the butterfat requirement must exceed 19 percent or does the certificate have to specify the exact percentage of butterfat?

     A. The certificate must specify the exact percentage of butterfat in cream required by the patient.

20. Q. May cream or cream products having butterfat in excess of 19 percent be sold to governmental agencies or institutions?

     A. No.

21. Q. May a farm family consume cream or cream products having a butterfat content in excess of 19 percent, if produced on the farm?

     A. Yes.

22. Q. May a farmer give cream or cream products testing more than 19 percent butterfat to another farmer?

     A. No. Cream or cream products having a butterfat content of more than 19 percent may not be given, sold, or delivered to another farmer unless such farmer is a handler according to the definition of this term in the Order.

23. Q. Is the sale or delivery of cream or cream products from one handler to another subject to the maximum butterfat provisions of the Order?

     A. No. Sales or deliveries of cream or cream products by one handler to another are not subject to the maximum butterfat provisions of the Order.

24. Q. A milk company gives each of its employees a bottle of cream containing more than 19 percent butterfat as a gift. Is this permissible under the Order?

     A. No. A gift to employees is considered a delivery in violation of the terms of the Order.

F

LIBRARY
CURRENT SERIAL RECORD
☆ JUN 9 1944 ☆
U. S. DEPARTMENT OF AGRICULTURE

WAR FOOD ADMINISTRATION

WFO 13
AMDT. 2
JUNE 2, 1944

[WFO 13, Amdt. 2]

PART 1401—DAIRY PRODUCTS

CREAM

War Food Order No. 13, as amended, 9 F.R. 4319 (formerly designated as Food Distribution Order No. 13, as originally issued by the Secretary of Agriculture on February 2, 1943, 8 F.R. 1479, as amended, 8 F.R. 11835), is further amended to read as follows:

§ 1401.13 *Restrictions with respect to cream*—(a) . *Definitions.* (1) "Person" means any individual, partnership, association, business trust, corporation, or any organized group of persons, whether incorporated or not.

(2) "Handler" means any person who engages in the business of transporting or processing milk or cream, or of manufacturing any dairy product. Such term shall not include persons who merely deliver milk or cream to consumers, institutional or otherwise.

(3) "Milk" means cow's milk.

(4) "Cream" means the class of food which is the sweet, fatty liquid or semiliquid separated from milk, with or without the addition thereto and the mixing therewith of sweet milk or sweet skim milk, irrespective of whether it is pasteurized or homogenized, and which contains not less than 18 percent of milk fat. Such term shall, for the purposes of this order, include, but not be restricted to, (i) light cream, coffee cream, table cream, whipping cream, heavy cream, plastic cream, sour cream, aerated cream, and any other cream by whatever name known; and (ii) reconstituted cream made from butter and one or more of the following ingredients: milk, skim milk, evaporated milk, condensed milk, cream, dried whole milk, dried skim milk, dried cream, or water.

(5) "Cream product" means cream to which there has been added, or which has been blended or compounded with, a culture, stabilizer, or like agent or ingredient; or with sugar, salt, condiments, spices, flavoring, or similar ingredients; whether or not the resultant product is pasteurized, homogenized, or sterilized.

(6) "Filled cream" means any milk, cream, or skim milk, whether or not condensed, evaporated, concentrated, powdered, dried, or desiccated, to which there has been added, or with which there has been blended or compounded, any fat or oil other than milk fat, so that the resulting product is an imitation of cream or in semblance thereof, whether or not such resulting product contains any other ingredient.

(7) "Milk fat," sometimes known as "butterfat," means the fat of milk; the proportionate content of such milk fat in milk or cream to be determined by the method prescribed in "Official and Tentative Methods of Analysis of the Association of Official Agricultural Chemists,"

Fifth Edition, 1940, page 267, under "Fat,—tient or the Babcock Method—Official."

(8) "Director" means the Director of Distribution, War Food Administration.

(9) "State" means any of the forty-eight States of the United States, the District of Columbia, or any Territory or Possession of the United States.

(b) *Restrictions.* (1) No person shall sell or deliver, except to a handler, any cream or cream product having a milk fat content in excess of 19 percent: *Provided,* That any person may sell or deliver cream having a milk fat content not exceeding by more than 1 percent the minimum milk fat content required by State law or administrative regulation in effect on November 25, 1942, in the State where such delivery is made.

(2) No person shall sell or deliver, except to a handler, any cream or cream product which has been fortified with, or to which there has been added, or with which there has been blended or compounded, evaporated milk, condensed milk, dried whole milk, or dried skim milk.

(3) No person shall, after July 31, 1944, sell or deliver filled cream having a total content of all oil and fat, including milk fat, in excess of 19 percent, but this shall not be construed to permit the manufacture, sale, or delivery of filled cream in violation of the Filled Milk Act (21 U. S. C., 1940 ed., 61–64).

(4) Notwithstanding the provisions of (b) (1) and (b) (2) hereof, any person may sell or deliver to any restaurant, hotel, or other public eating place any cream or cream product having a milk fat content in excess of that permitted by (b) (1) hereof or any cream or cream product of the type described in (b) (2) hereof, if the purchaser certifies in writing to the seller that such cream or cream product is to be used in the manufacture of frozen dairy foods in accordance with the provisions of War Food Order No. 8, issued by the War Food Administrator.

(5) No restaurant, hotel, or other public eating place shall use any cream or cream product having a milk fat content in excess of 19 percent, except in the manufacture of frozen dairy foods in accordance with the provisions of said War Food Order No. 8: *Provided,* That any such restaurant, hotel, or other public eating place may use for all purposes cream having a milk fat content not exceeding by more than 1 percent the minimum milk fat content required by State law or administrative regulation in effect on November 25, 1942, in the State where such takes place.

(c) *Exemptions.* (1) Notwithstanding the provisions of (b) hereof, any person may sell or deliver to or for any patient, or to any establishment engaged in the care and treatment of the sick, cream of such milk fat content, and in such quantities, as may be necessary for supervised medical treatment of such pa-

tients of such establishment: *Provided,* That such person is supplied with a written statement from the patient's physician or, in the case of an establishment engaged in the care and treatment of the sick, from a responsible official thereof who is a practicing physician, and such written statement shall be valid for a period of not to exceed sixty days from the date of issuance and shall specify (i) the milk fat content of cream required for such use, (ii) the daily quantity of such cream, and (iii) with regard to the necessity of such cream for supervised medical treatment: *Provided further,* That such written statement shall not be valid for obtaining such cream after July 31, 1944, unless approved by the public health officer, or the secretary of the county medical society, of the municipality or county wherein such patient resides or such establishment is located.

(2) Upon application by one or more persons in any marketing area and after demonstration to the satisfaction of the Director that compliance with the provisions of (b) (1) hereof will not tend to conserve milk fat for war and essential civilian needs, the Director may grant an exemption from the provisions of (b) (1) hereof to any or all persons in such area.

(d) *Audits and inspections.* The Director shall be entitled to make such audit or inspection of the books, records and other writings, premises or stocks of cream, cream products, or filled cream of any person, and to make such investigations, as may be necessary or appropriate, in the Director's discretion, to the enforcement or administration of the provisions of this order.

(e) *Records and reports.* (1) The Director shall be entitled to obtain such information from, and require such reports and the keeping of such records by, any person, as may be necessary or appropriate, in the Director's discretion, to the enforcement or administration of the provisions of this order.

(2) Every person subject to this order shall, for at least two years (or for such period of time as the Director may designate), maintain an accurate record of his transactions in cream, cream products, and filled cream.

(f) *Petition for relief from hardship.* Any person affected by this order, who considers that compliance herewith would work an exceptional and unreasonable hardship on him, may file a petition for relief with the Regional Director of Distribution, serving the area (8 F.R. 15764) in which such person resides or does business. Petitions for such relief shall be in writing and shall set forth all pertinent facts and the nature of the relief sought. The Regional Director may take any action with reference to such petition which is consistent with the authority delegated to him by the Director. If the petitioner is dissatisfied with the action taken by the Regional Director on the petition, he shall, by requesting the Regional Director therefor, obtain a review of such action by the Director. The Director may, after said review, take such action as he deems appropriate, and such action shall be final. The provisions of this paragraph (f) shall not be construed to deprive the Director of authority to consider originally any petition for relief from hardship submitted in accordance herewith. The Director may consider any such petition and take such action with reference thereto as he deems appropriate, and such action shall be final.

(g) *Violations.* Any person who violates any provision of this order may, in accordance with the applicable procedure, be prohibited from receiving, making any deliveries of, or using cream, cream products, and filled cream, or any other material subject to priority or allocation control by any governmental agency. In addition, any person who wilfully violates any provision of this order is guilty of a crime and may be prose-

cuted under any and all applicable laws. Further, civil action may be instituted to enforce any liability or duty created by, or to enjoin any violation of, any provision of this order.

(h) *Delegation of authority.* The administration of this order and the powers vested in the War Food Administrator, insofar as such powers relate to the administration of this order, are hereby delegated to the Director. The Director is authorized to redelegate to any employee of the United States Department of Agriculture any or all of the authority vested in him by this order.

(i) *Communications.* All reports required to be filed hereunder and all communications concerning this order shall be addressed to the Regional Director of Distribution, War Food Administration, serving the area (8 F.R. 15764) in which the person affected by the order resides or does business.

(j) *Territorial extent.* This order shall apply to the forty-eight States of the United States, the District of Columbia, and the Territories and Possessions of the United States.

(k) *Effective date.* This order shall become effective at 12:01 a. m., e. w. t., June 7, 1944. With respect to any violation of War Food Order No. 13, as amended, or rights accrued, liabilities incurred, or appeals taken under said order, as amended, prior to the effective date hereof, said War Food Order No. 13, as amended, shall be deemed to continue in full force and effect for the purpose of sustaining any proper suit, action, or other proceeding with respect to any such violation, right, liability, or appeal.

NOTE: All record-keeping requirements of this order have been approved by, and subsequent reporting and record-keeping requirements will be subject to the approval of, Bureau of the Budget in accordance with the Federal Reports Act of 1942.

(E.O. 9280, 7 F.R. 10179; E.O. 9322, 8 F.R. 3807; E.O. 9334, 8 F.R. 5423; E.O. 9392, 8 F.R. 14783).

Issued this 2d day of June 1944.

ASHLEY SELLERS,
Assistant War Food Administrator.

War Food Administration
Summary to WFO 13 Am. 2.

The War Food Administration has announced that beginning August 1 all prescriptions for heavy cream must be approved by a local public health officer or the secretary of a county medical society.

At the same time, the WFA tightened its ban on the distribution of heavy cream by extending the limitation to include not only fluid cream and cream products, but cream substitutes—that is, cream to which some oil or fat other than milkfat has been added. Beginning August 1, 1944, the sale or delivery of so-called "filled" cream, containing more than 19 percent of all kinds of fat, will be prohibited. WFA officials said the action represents a further effort to save milk solids for more essential wartime uses.

WFO 13 prohibits the sale of heavy cream containing more than 19% butter-

fat in order to conserve milk for more essential wartime uses, such as butter and skim milk powder. The order provided, however, that physicians might prescribe such cream in cases where it was important to the health of their patients. During the past few months, medical societies and local officials have reported to the WFA that some physicians have freely prescribed heavy cream. Today's action is expected to limit the use of rich cream to the rare cases where it may be required.

Effective June 7, today's action also:

(1) Broadens the present definition of cream products to include aerated (air-expanded) cream, reconstituted cream, and those cream products to which sugar, condiments, spices, flavoring or similar ingredients have been added. This restriction is designed to prevent dealers from marketing a product containing more than the allowed percentage of butterfat by varying its composition slightly.

(2) Tightens present restrictions on heavy cream or cream products by specifically prohibiting their sale to or use by hotels, restaurants and other public eating places, except for making ice cream. (Under another order—WFO 8—the use of cream or other milk solids in the production of frozen dairy foods is limited.)

In California, the District of Columbia, Minnesota, Montana and Nevada, where the milk-fat content of fluid cream is required by law to exceed 18 percent, dealers may deliver cream having a milk-fat content not exceeding the State legal minimum by more than 1 percent.

(These provisions are contained in Amendment 2 to WFO 13. This amendment is effective June 7, 1944, with the exception of the provisions regarding filled cream and approval of physicians certificates by local public-health officers of county medical societies. These are effective August 1, 1944.)

GPO—WFA 696—p. 2

[WFO 13, Amdt. 5]

PART 1401—DAIRY PRODUCTS

CREAM

War Food Order No. 13 (8 F.R. 1479) issued on February 2, 1943, as amended (8 F.R. 11835, 9 F.R. 4321, 4319, 6145, 9584, 10 F.R. 103), is hereby further amended to read as follows:

§ 1401.13 *Restrictions with respect to cream*—(a) *Definitions.* (1) "Person" means any individual, partnership, association, business trust, corporation, or any organized group of persons, whether incorporated or not.

(2) "Handler" means (i) any person who engages in the business of transporting or processing milk or cream, or of manufacturing any dairy product, or (ii) any person who produces filled cream for sale as such or for use as an ingredient in the manufacture or preparation of food products for sale. Such term shall not include persons, such as peddlers, vendors, or retail stores, who merely deliver milk or cream to consumers, institutional or otherwise.

(3) "Milk" means cow's milk.

(4) "Cream" means the class of food which is the fatty liquid or semi-liquid separated from milk, with or without the addition thereto and the mixing therewith of milk or skim milk, irrespective of whether it is pasteurized or homogenized, and which contains not less than 18 percent of milk fat. In addition, such term shall, for the purposes of this order, include, but not be restricted to (i) light cream, coffee cream, table cream, whipping cream, whipped cream, heavy cream, plastic cream, sour cream, aerated cream, frozen cream, and any other cream by whatever name known; (ii) reconstituted cream made from two or more of the following ingredients: butter, milk, skim milk, evaporated milk, condensed milk, cream, dried whole milk, dried skim milk, dried cream, and water; and (iii) whey cream.

(5) "Cream product" means cream to which there has been added, or which has been blended or compounded with, a culture, stabilizer, or like agent or ingredient; or with sugar, salt, condiments, spices, flavoring, or similar ingredients; whether or not the resultant product is pasteurized, homogenized, or sterilized.

(6) "Filled cream" means any milk, cream, or skim milk, or a mixture of milk, cream, and skim milk, whether or not condensed, evaporated, concentrated, powdered, dried, or desiccated, to which there has been added, or with which there has been blended or compounded, any fat or oil other than milk fat, so that the resulting product is an imitation of cream or in semblance thereof, whether or not such resulting product contains any other ingredient, provided that it has a total content of all oil and fat including, milk fat, in excess of 19 percent.

(7) "Milk fat," sometimes known as "butterfat," means the fat of milk; the proportionate content of such milk fat in milk or cream to be determined by the method prescribed in "Official and Tentative Methods of Analysis of the Association of Official Agricultural Chemists," Fifth Edition, 1940, page 287, under "Fat, Babcock Method—Official."

(8) "Milk solids" means the solids of milk and consists of milk fat and milk solids-not-fat (sometimes referred to as serum solids).

(9) "Base period" means (i) the calendar month of May 1944 in the case of a handler who produced less than 100 gallons of filled cream during any calendar month from April 1, 1943, to March 31, 1944, inclusive, and who produced filled cream, in any quantity, during May 1944; and (ii) the period from April 1, 1943, to March 31, 1944, inclusive, in the case of all other handlers.

(10) "Quota period" means the calendar month of February 1945, or any calendar month thereafter.

(11) "Monthly base," applicable to any quota period, means (i) for a handler whose base period is May 1944, the pounds of milk solids utilized by him in the production of filled cream during such base period; and (ii) for a handler whose base period is the period from April 1, 1943, to March 31, 1944, inclusive, the pounds of milk solids utilized by such handler in the production of filled cream during the corresponding calendar month of such base period.

(12) "Quota" means the pounds of milk solids which a handler may utilize in the production of filled cream during a quota period.

(13) "Director" means the Director of Marketing Services, War Food Administration.

(14) "State" means any of the forty-eight States of the United States, the District of Columbia, or any Territory or Possession of the United States.

(b) *Restrictions on cream and cream products.* (1) No person shall sell or deliver, except to a handler, any cream or cream product having a milk fat content in excess of 19 percent: *Provided,* That any person may sell or deliver cream having a milk fat content not exceeding by more than 1 percent the minimum milk fat content required by State law or administrative regulation in effect on November 25, 1942, in the State where such delivery is made.

(2) No person shall sell or deliver, except to a handler, any cream or cream product which has been fortified with, or to which there has been added, or with which there has been blended or compounded, evaporated milk, condensed milk, dried whole milk, or dried skim milk.

(3) No handler shall use any cream or cream product having a milk fat content in excess of 19 percent, except in the processing of milk or cream, or in the manufacture of a dairy product, or in the production of filled cream: *Provided,* That any handler may use for all purposes cream having a milk fat content not exceeding by more than 1 percent the minimum milk fat content required by State law or administrative regulation in effect on November 25, 1942, in the State where such use takes place.

(4) Notwithstanding the provisions of (b) (1) and (b) (2) hereof, any person may sell or deliver to any restaurant, hotel, bakery, or similar establishment any cream or cream product having a milk fat content in excess of that permitted by (b) (1) hereof or any cream or cream product of the type described in (b) (2) hereof, if the purchaser certifies in writing to the seller that such cream or cream product is to be used in the manufacture of frozen dairy foods in accordance with the provisions of War Food Order No. 8 (8 F.R. 953; 9 F.R. 4321, 4319), as amended.

(5) No restaurant, hotel, bakery, or similar establishment shall use any cream or cream product having a milk fat content in excess of 19 percent, except in the manufacture of frozen dairy foods in accordance with the provisions of said War Food Order No. 8, as amended: *Provided,* That any such restaurant, hotel, bakery, or similar establishment may use for all purposes cream having a milk fat content not exceeding by more than 1 percent the minimum milk fat content required by State law or administrative regulation in effect on November 25, 1942, in the State where such use takes place.

(c) *Restrictions on the utilization of milk solids in filled cream.* (1) Except as otherwise specified by the Director no handler shall during any quota period, utilize in the production of filled cream a quantity of milk solids in excess of his quota.

(2) The quota for each handler in each quota period shall be 75 percent of the monthly base.

(3) The Director may, in the event of the sale of a handler's business, transfer the monthly base from the selling handler to the buying handler, upon application by either handler.

(4) The monthly base and the quota shall be in terms of pounds of milk solids. The quantity of milk solids-not-fat in cream or milk used in the production of filled cream shall be computed by multiplying the pounds of skim milk contained in such cream or milk by 0.09375. The quantity of milk solids-not-fat in fluid skim milk used in the production of filled cream shall be computed by multiplying the pounds of skim milk so used by 0.09375. The milk solids-not-fat content of other products utilized in the production of filled cream shall be computed in accordance with conversion factors to be determined by the Director, but, until such determination is made, handlers may use conversion factors normally used by them.

(d) *Exemptions.* (1) Notwithstanding the provisions of (b) hereof, any person may sell or deliver to or for any patient, or to any establishment engaged in the care and treatment of the sick, cream of such milk fat content, and in such quantities, as may be necessary for supervised medical treatment of such patient or the patients of such establishment: *Provided,* That such person is supplied with a written statement from the patient's physician or, in the case of an establishment engaged in the care and treatment of the sick, from a responsible official thereof who is a practicing physician, and such written statement shall be valid for a period of not to exceed sixty days from the date of issuance and shall specify (i) the milk fat content of cream required for such use, (ii) the daily quantity of such cream, and (iii) with regard to the necessity of such cream for supervised medical treatment: *Provided further,* That such written statement shall not be valid for obtaining such cream unless approved by a public health officer who is a physician, or by the secretary of the county medical society of the county wherein such patient resides or such establishment is located.

(2) Upon application by one or more persons in any area or region and after demonstration to the satisfaction of the Director that compliance with the provisions of (b) (1) hereof will not tend to conserve milk fat for war and essential civilian needs, or upon the initiative of the Director, the Director may grant an exemption from the provisions of (b) (1) hereof to any or all persons in such area or region, or to any or all persons in any area or region specified by the Director.

(e) *Audits and inspections.* The Director shall be entitled to make such audit or inspection of the books, records and other writings, premises or stocks of cream, cream products, or filled cream of any person, and to make such investigations, as may be necessary or appropriate, in the Director's discretion, to the enforcement or administration of the provisions of this order.

(f) *Records and reports.* (1) Each person who produces filled cream on February 7, 1945, shall, within 10 calendar days after such date, and each person who starts to produce filled cream after the aforesaid date shall, within 10 calendar days after he starts to produce such filled cream, submit to the Director, in writing, the following information: (i) the total volume of filled cream, in number of gallons, produced by him during each calendar month from April 1, 1943, to March 31, 1944, inclusive, and during May 1944; and (ii) for each calendar month of his base period, a list of all of the ingredients used by him in the production of filled cream; the volume of filled cream, in number of gallons, produced by him; the percent of milk fat contained in such filled cream; the percent of all oil and fat, including milk fat, contained in such filled cream; and the total pounds of milk solids utilized by him in the production of such filled cream.

(2) The Director shall be entitled to obtain such additional information from, and require such reports and the keeping of such records by, any person, as may be necessary or appropriate, in the Director's discretion, to the enforcement or administration of the provisions of this order.

(3) Every person subject to this order shall, for at least two years (or for such period of time as the Director may designate), maintain an accurate record of his transactions in cream, cream products, and filled cream.

(g) *Petition for relief from hardship.* Any person affected by this order who considers that compliance herewith would work an exceptional or unreasonable hardship on him may file a petition for relief with the Order Administrator. Such petition shall be addressed to Order Administrator, War Food Order No. 13, Dairy and Poultry Branch, Office of Marketing Services, War Food Administration, Washington 25, D. C. Petition for such relief shall be in writing and shall set forth all pertinent facts and the nature of the relief sought. The Order Administrator may take any action with reference to such petition which is consistent with the authority delegated to him by the Director. If the petitioner is dissatisfied with the action taken by the Order Administrator on the petition, he shall obtain, by requesting the Order Administrator therefor, a review of such action by the Director. The Director may, after said review, take such action as he deems appropriate, and such action shall be final. The provisions of this paragraph (g) shall not be construed to deprive the Director of authority to consider originally any petition for relief from hardship submitted in accordance herewith. The Director may consider any such petition and take such action with reference thereto that he deems appropriate, and such action shall be final.

(h) *Violations.* Any person who violates any provision of this order may, in accordance with the applicable procedure, be prohibited from receiving, making any deliveries of, or using the material subject to priority or allocation control pursuant to this order. In addition, any person who wilfully violates any provision of this order is guilty of a crime and may be prosecuted under any and all applicable laws. Further, civil action may be instituted to enforce any liability or duty created by, or to enjoin any violation of, any provision of this order.

(i) *Delegation of authority.* The administration of this order and the powers vested in the War Food Administrator, insofar as such powers relate to the administration of this order, are hereby delegated to the Director. The Director is authorized to redelegate to any employee of the United States Department of Agriculture any or all of the authority vested in him by this order; and one such employee shall be designated by the Director to serve as Order Administrator.

(j) *Communications.* All reports required to be filed hereunder and all communications concerning this order shall, unless otherwise provided herein or in instructions issued by the Director, be addressed to the Order Administrator, War Food Order No. 13, Dairy and Poultry Branch, Office of Marketing Services. War Food Administration, Washington 25, D. C.

(k) *Territorial extent.* This order shall apply to the forty-eight States of the United States, the District of Columbia, and the Territories and Possessions of the United States.

(l) *Effective date.* This order shall become effective at 12:01 a. m., e. w. t., February 7, 1945. With respect to violations, rights accrued, liabilities incurred, or appeals taken under said War Food Order No. 13, as amended, prior to the effective time of the provisions hereof, the provisions of said War Food Order No. 13, as amended, in effect prior to the effective time hereof shall be deemed to continue in full force and effect for the purpose of sustaining any proper suit, action, or other proceeding with regard to any such violation, right, liability, or appeal.

NOTE: All reporting and record-keeping requirements of this order have been approved by, and subsequent reporting and record-keeping requirements will be subject to the approval of, Bureau of the Budget in accordance with the Federal Reports Act of 1942.

(E.O. 9280, 7 F.R. 10179; E.O. 9322, 8 F.R. 3807; E.O. 9334, 8 F.R. 5423; E.O. 9392, 8 F.R. 14783)

Issued this 6th day of February 1945.

ASHLEY SELLERS,
Assistant War Food Administrator.

War Food Administration
Office of Marketing Services
Washington 25, D. C.

Official Business